Advance Praise for

Counting Up the Olive Tree: A Palestine Number Book

"Golbarg Bashi, cleverly uses the game of football, that is unifying to the world, that is relatable and fun, watched by all and played by all to connect with people, while still giving the readers an insight to the reality of what life is like in Palestine. After her success with *P is for Palestine*, in these short stories, we are being educated in a way that is important for people to see the humanity in those people who are in distress. Showcasing their bravery and their courage, to resist in ways that are peaceful and full of promise and hope."

—**Joudie Kalla,** Palestinian-British author of *Palestine on A Plate*

"A dazzling follow up to *P is for Palestine*. *Counting Up the Olive Tree* is a jamboree of colors and childhood exuberance rooted in the heart of Palestine. An infectious delight for young readers and parents alike."

—**Remi Kanazi,** Palestinian-American poet and author of *Before the Next Bomb Drops*

"There are many different ways to tell a story and shed light on profound truths about the human condition. Golbarg Bashi brilliantly and whimsically uses football — one thing that unites the world, with another, the fierce urgency of protecting that which we all share equally — this precious planet — all to highlight the importance of dignity and love. Makes me wish I could have read this and shared it with my friends as a kid."

—**Ahmed Shihab-Eldin,** Palestinian-American Emmy-nominated journalist

"This welcome book will charm children, and while increasing their understanding of numbers, will also help them to learn about Palestine, filling a gap for many families who want to broaden their children's horizons."

—**Rashid Khalidi,** Edward Said Professor of Modern Arab Studies at Columbia University

"*Counting Up the Olive Tree: A Palestine Number Book* teaches numbers in a context of resistance to the destruction of that most symbolic icon of Palestine: the olive tree... Many different emotions welled up in me as I looked at this book. I thoroughly enjoyed the uplifting storyline, as well as the cheerful illustrations. 'Delightful' kept coming up as the most appropriate adjective. But also, empowering. Inspiring. I absolutely loved the objective statement, a matter-of-fact sober observation nevertheless pointing towards a hopeful outcome, 'the land yet to be free.' And mostly, I was grateful for Golbarg Bashi, who not only did not cave in after the hate she received upon publishing "*P is for Palestine*," but instead went ahead and authored another book for us. I have ordered a few copies myself. You can too. So we can save our olive trees, in the land which shall be free."

—**Dr. Nada Elia,** Palestinian-American author and journalist

"Golbarg Bashi does it again - shedding new light on stereotypes, and starting where it counts."

—**Najwa Najjar,** Award-winning Palestinian filmmaker

"What a beautiful way Golbarg Bashi uses to teach children the deep rooted significance and love we as Palestinians have for our olive trees. I am in awe of the vibrant colors and excitement of the children as they learn the numbers while sitting on the strong branches of the olive tree. Well done to Dr. Bashi as an independent author and publisher and as a sequel to *P is for Palestine*!"

—**The Rev. Khader El-Yateem,** Palestinian-born Pastor and Community Organizer based in the U.S.

Dedicated to Bill Martin, Jr.

Golbarg Bashi

***

Oh all you olive trees of Palestine
Address all the abundance of your shades
To me:
To this lonesome traveler
Having just returned
From the vicinity of Mount Sinai
Feverish with
The heat of the Divine Speech–

~Sohrab Sepehri, "Traveler" (1965)

Translation from the original Persian by Hamid Dabashi

Counting Up the Olive Tree: A Palestine Number Book
Author: Golbarg Bashi
Illustrator: Nabi H. Ali
Layout: KB Studio
Copyright © 2019, Golbarg Bashi
All rights reserved under International and American Copyright Conventions.
Published in the United States by Dr. Bashi™, New York, NY.
www.drbashi.com/books
ISBN-10: 0-9990020-3-1 | ISBN-13: 978-0-9990020-3-2
Dr. Bashi™ Diverse Children's Books Series, 2019
Printed in the United States of America
www.drbashi.com

COUNTING UP THE OLIVE TREE
A PALESTINE NUMBER BOOK

by
GOLBARG BASHI

Illustrated by
NABI H. ALI

Someone goofy once said:
"Kids don't play where their trees aren't spared."
But that's just silly.

Call it soccer, call it football,
One way or another, let's play ball!

And when the woodcutter comes again to cut down what's now
the kids' last olive tree,
the players will plea:

"Please don't cut our precious tree in our land yet to be free!"

Making the woodcutter shudder, picking up his axe,
while wanting to first eat lunch, rest, and relax.

Relax, he does and falls asleep.
That's when our heroic numbers say:
"the time has come for us to leap!"

Player number 1 tells player number 2,
get hold of number 3
who tells 4,
"we must protect the last olive tree,
all of us and some more."

6

"Ya'llah says 5
to 6 7 and 8.
"Let's climb up the last olive tree.
And wait!"

Tlick - Tlock Tlick - Tlock
Will there be enough time?

Up goes player 9
up the last olive tree,
with 10 and 11
on their way
up the last olive tree
which has to stay!

Tlick - Tlock Tlick – Tlock!
Will there be enough time?

9

10

Look who's coming!

11

The players from en-Na'ime!

1 2 3 4
And 5 6 7 8.

Still more—look 9 is here!
And 10 11—do you hear?

The whole team!
Climbing up the last olive tree!

13

14

Tlick - Tlock Tlick – Tlock!

Zzzz

Snoring cracking humming and roaring!

Wait!
The woodcutter is waking up,
no longer snoring!

16

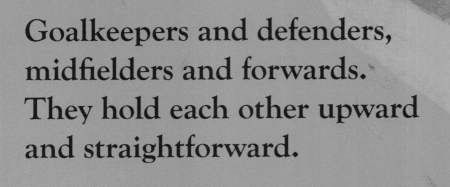

Goalkeepers and defenders,
midfielders and forwards.
They hold each other upward
and straightforward.

"We'll defend you, and the last olive tree"
cry the defenders in the land yet to be free!

17

The 2 goalkeepers use their bare hands,
behind the 4 defenders.

4 outside fullbacks are on the left, and 4 right flanks are on the sides of the last olive tree in Palestine!

21

The 4 center forwards are ready.
And the 4 midfielders are extra strong and steady!
Tlick - Tlock Tlick – Tlock!

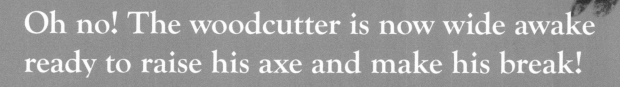

Oh no! The woodcutter is now wide awake
ready to raise his axe and make his break!

But wait!
When the woodcutter sees all the players
and their numbers,
he begins to count them, woken up from
his slumber.

28

There is much strategizing, criticizing, galvanizing,
that the woodcutter is forced to say: "I should be
apologizing!"

"You bet you should," cry the players,
to each and every one of your neighbors!

The woodcutter says sorry to
players 1 2 3 4 5 6 7 8 9 10 and 11

The woodcutter also says sorry to
players 11 10 9 8 7 6 5 4 3 2 and 1

The woodcutter has to say sorry to
the players' mamas and papas
their grandmas and grandpas,
their uncles and aunts and cousins...

By the time the sun tells the moon
of all that happened by the last olive
tree that afternoon,
the woodcutter had

said a whole lot of sorry.
And he had a lot less to worry.
Can you guess just how many?
Only if you're not in a hurry!

40

Previously in the Dr. Bashi™ Diverse Children's Books Series

P is for Palestine: A Palestine Alphabet Book

"*P is for Palestine* teaches children the alphabet using Palestinian references."

—*New York Daily News*

"I was excited to spot *P is for Palestine* by Golbarg Bashi. The book is fantastic on so many different levels: it features a little girl with curly black hair, big eyes and brown skin; the illustrations are gorgeous; and it teaches the alphabet through egalitarian and multi-cultural words from both Arabic and English."

—Radhika Sainath, *American writer and civil rights lawyer*

"It's not every day that people protest a children's book, '*Huckleberry Finn*,' '*Harry Potter*,' Harper Lee's '*Go Set a Watchman*' and now '*P is for Palestine*.'"

—Shira Hanau, *Jewish Week Newspaper*

"Adorable alphabet book that's flying off our shelves. Readers will have to patiently wait in line to buy multiple copies of *P is for Palestine: A Palestine Alphabet Book* for the children in their lives, as well as the children they want to reach in libraries and schools across the country."

—*Washington Report on Middle East Affairs*

The "children's book that claims 'Christmas is a Palestinian festival' and that Jesus was an Abrahamic prophet born in a Palestinian city Bethlehem . . . [it] should be outright banned from American bookstores."

—*Fox News*

"A new twist on the genre aims to teach kids the ABCs of Palestinian culture."

–Haaretz

"New York history professor and author of the book *P is for Palestine* helps children cut through the political haystack."

–The Arab American News

"In New York City, store clerks were reportedly forced to hide copies of *P is for Palestine* behind the cash register. Like something out of a Soviet-era spy novel, you could only get a copy if you knew to ask for it."

–Literary Hub

"Only Salman Rushdie's Satanic Verses (1988) has caused the same stir as *P is for Palestine* (2017) in New York City."

–Jewish Week Newspaper

"*P is for Palestine* provides much needed representation of Palestinian culture in children's literature."

–Columbia University Students for Justice in Palestine

"This brightly-illustrated book reveals a side of Palestine that is often hidden, by highlighting its rich religious heritage."

–Palestine in America

"Cheerful little book, in which a curly-haired young girl guides us through her homeland. A genuine celebration of the historical diversity of Palestine, the book does a stellar job of reminding Westerners, many of whom believe Christianity is a Western religion, that it is Palestine that is the birthplace of Christianity."

–Dr. Nada Elia, Palestinian author and journalist

"The book presents a beautifully illustrated, unapologetically proud narrative of Palestinian identity. *P is for Palestine* is exactly the kind of positive reinforcement needed by children whose identity is constantly under attack...Every child could benefit from learning about Palestine in a positive and uplifting way . . . [a] gift of learning about Palestine in the context of working for freedom, justice and equality."

–Dr. Yousef Munayyer, US Campaign for Palestinian Rights

"When does a children's book get coverage in the New York Post ('Page Six,' no less), the Forward, Ha'aretz, the New York Daily News, and Breitbart? [T]eaching and learning about Palestine has been a sore spot for Zionists. The book provides an ocular target for their existential anxiety."

—Dr. Steven Salaita, *Palestinian-American academic and writer*

"*P is for Palestine* is the glorification of the Palestinian intifada."

—Rabbi Ammiel Hirsch, *Stephen Wise Free Synagogue, New York*

"The first ABC picture book about Palestine is definitely an important book for people of Palestinian heritage who want to share it with their children."

—*Intellectual Freedom of the American Library Association*

"*P is for Palestine* is a children's book that teaches about justice and resistance. Solidarity with the oppressed is a value we must do our best to model for the next generations. For kids, the love of books and reading is essential. Palestinian kids, who are too often robbed of their childhoods by a brutal occupation regime, deserve the same right to play, learn, read and laugh that any other children enjoy."

—John Leslie, *American writer and activist*

"*P is for Palestine* is a colorful manifestation of all that is beautiful about the land of my parents and ancestors. This book is a gift that takes you on a journey of love, life and resilience; the virtues of my beloved Palestine."

—Linda Sarsour, *Award-winning Palestinian American activist*

"You will fall in love with this innovative, much needed, and beautifully illustrated Palestinian alphabet book. Highly recommended!"

—Dr. Jack G. Shaheen (1935 – 2017) author of *Reel Bad Arabs: How Hollywood Vilifies a People*

"This powerful book will prove to be pivotal for so many young Palestinians on their search for identity and belonging, and will introduce countless others to a place and people that have been marginalized for too long in their struggle for equality. I can't wait to buy copies for my niece, and her friends. P is for 'Palestine', and also for 'Proud.'"

—Ahmed Shihab-Eldin, *Palestinian-American Emmy-nominated journalist*

"G for GREAT . . .
P for PEACE IN PALESTINE."

—Dr. Marwan Bishara, Award-wining *Palestinian author and broadcaster*

"Golbarg Bashi's *P is for Palestine* is a moving journey of alphabetical letters becoming a bridge, a boat that connects us to our homeland and our heritage, while yearning for freedom & peace in Palestine."

—Rula Jebreal, *Award-winning Palestinian author*

"I wish I had a book like this when I was a child! Fantastic and fun . . . a great way to show children another world and open their minds. It's especially exciting to me as a Palestinian as I always want to find ways to show my baby she can feel proud of her culture and have fun at the same time. Colorful, truly original and a delight for young and old!"

—Annemarie Jacir, *Academy Award nominated Palestinian Filmmaker*

"I'm so happy to live in a world where a book like *P is for Palestine* exists. If I had had something like this as a child, I would have felt so much less alone and so much more interested in my culture, instead of wondering why no one else seemed to know the words that were so comforting and real to me. I cannot wait to give a copy to my niece, nephew, and every other little Arab American child, who will not only be able to learn from this book, but will also be able to feel proud of where she is from, and, consequently, rooted deeply in the world."

—Najla Said, *Palestinian-American playwright and author*

"Golbarg Bashi takes children (and parents) into Palestine, illustrated beautifully with Golrokh Nafisi's drawings. *P is for Palestine* is a must for anyone who grew up with fragmented past and is looking to changing today's stereotypes."

—Najwa Najjar, *Award-winning Palestinian filmmaker*

"Palestine is our story, and our story begins with the alphabet.
Every letter a direction. Stunningly illustrated.
A dream-book for all ages."

—Nathalie Handal, *Award-winning Palestinian poet and writer*

"A book for our children that teaches self-love and pride. A book for our friends that shares a central piece of our lives. A book for ourselves that sings without apology: *P is for Palestine* and all of its wonders that make it home."

—Noura Erakat, *Palestinian-American human rights attorney*

44

Golbarg Bashi is an Upper West Side Mama, a children's author and the founder of Dr. Bashi™, an independent woman-minority owned social justice publisher of diverse children's books based in Manhattan, New York. She was born in southern Iran, raised in Sweden, and educated in the U.K. and U.S. where she received her Ph.D. in Middle Eastern Studies and Gender from Columbia University. Growing up, she was widely exposed to the strong tradition of progressive children's literature in *Persian*, *Swedish*, and *English*. Her childhood experiences of the Iraq-Iran war and life in Sweden as a refugee have turned her into an advocate for diversity in children's literature and media. In 2016, Golbarg Bashi was nominated by the U.S. toy industry "*Wonder Woman Award*" in the Designer/Inventor category for advancing early childhood education together with her colleague, the acclaimed typographer Koroush Beigpour, for languages using the Arabic and Persian-scripts. Her first children's book, *P is for Palestine: A Palestine Alphabet Book* (November 2017), sold out within days and is now in its 7th print (2019). In March 2019, her first Persian-language children's book (soon also available in English), titled *Saving Maahi: An Iranian Spring Solstice New Year Story about Nowruz* was launched to great critical acclaim in Iran: www. drbashi.com/books

Nabi H. Ali is a Tamil-American illustrator who enjoys creating diverse works that showcase an array of cultures and peoples. His interest in illustrative works started when he realized he could help create representation in the arts and in media for minorities, and he is very passionate about working with characters that he would have liked to see when he was a kid. Mr. Ali is aspiring to become a visual development artist for animation alongside his pursuit of illustration and has worked for studios like Wild Canary Animation as a freelance character designer. Usually, he illustrates digitally, but he also has a secret love of inks, color pencil, and acrylic paints. His favorite quality in art is experimenting with color and what the right colors can do to make a piece of art magical. Mr. Ali's hobbies include drawing (of course), doll collecting, reading, learning about South Asian mythology and folklore, and researching history. For more information about his work, please visit: https://nabihaiderali.myportfolio.com

Publisher's Note

After the extraordinary success of *P is for Palestine: A Palestine Alphabet Book*, Golbarg Bashi has teamed up with the gifted American artist Nabi H. Ali to publish *Counting Up the Olive Tree: A Palestine Number Book* —a social justice homage to Bill Martin Jr. and his *Chicka Chicka Boom Boom* (1989), a legendary classic children's book we love—for what could possibly be equally important to knowing the letters of the alphabet? The numbers of course!

Counting Up the Olive Tree: A Palestine Number Book is a rhythmic, earth-friendly adventure where little Palestinian football (soccer) players save an olive tree. Our book aims to bring young Palestinians to their rightful place in the English-speaking children's literature, and remind us all of the importance of play and the protection of the environment in all children's lives and to help them practice counting the numbers (cultivating their math skills).

The tradition of number books goes back at least a century—helping children become familiar with numbers and basic math skills well before they start formal education. There are currently countless number books about themes and countries in the world— informing children about any number of topics, nations and cultures other than their own by also cultivating basic math skills. *Canada 1 2 3*; *We All Went on Safari: A Counting Journey Through Tanzania*; etc. But none about or for Palestine in English. Until now!

We were able to publish this second book in the *Dr. Bashi™ Diverse Children's Books Series* by partially financing its publication through the crowd-fundraising platform *LaunchGood.com* which allowed the generous Palestinian-American community and progressives to pre-purchase our book in advance. We are grateful for their support and trust in our vision.

For decades, the U.S. children's book publishing industry, right here in our hometown New York City, has actively erased and barred the slightest trace of Palestinian children's names and stories and thus denied this otherwise universal truth to generations of American children. Voices speaking on behalf of Palestinian freedom have been suppressed whether they be in a theatre play, a music concert, in a school or university classroom or even the publication of a small children's ABC book financed through a long and modest crowd-fundraiser. We know this firsthand as our own small contribution, the publication of our *P is for Palestine: A Palestine Alphabet Book* in 2017 was and continues to be met with astonishing levels of attacks, resulting in the virtual banning of our book in American bookstores and libraries (forced on by actual threats of financial boycott and/or violence by Israel Advocates on us and American institutions and businesses). The complete silence of institutions such as *Pen America* and *The Society of Children's Book Writers and Illustrators (SCBWI)* speaks loudly of their complicity.

We continue to rely on grassroots support to help enable us, a proudly woman-minority owned publisher, to have the freedom and independence to bring empowering social justice, educational books to children world-wide!

To donate to Dr. Bashi™ fund for the publication of our *Diverse Children's Books Series*, you may make your financial contribution to one of the following two accounts:

paypal.me/drbashi

venmo.com/drbashi

May, 2019
New York City